EMMANUEL JOSEPH

Soul of the Soil, A Journey Through Art, Mental Health, and Ecological Awakening

Contents

1

Chapter 1: The Canvas of Life

Life is a grand canvas, and every individual paints their unique masterpiece. In a small village nestled in the mountains, a young artist named Aisha found solace in nature's beauty. Her paintings depicted serene landscapes, vibrant flowers, and towering trees, each stroke infused with her emotions. One day, she met an elderly man, Kofi, who shared his wisdom on the healing power of art. Kofi's stories of overcoming trauma through painting inspired Aisha to embrace her creativity, leading her on a journey of self-discovery and healing.

Aisha's journey began with simple sketches of the flowers in her garden. As she spent more time outdoors, she noticed how the colors of the flowers changed with the seasons. She captured these changes in her art, finding peace and joy in the process. One day, while painting a particularly vibrant sunset, Aisha encountered Kofi, who was also an artist. Kofi had experienced great loss in his life, but he found solace in painting. He shared his story with Aisha, explaining how art had helped him heal and find a new purpose.

Inspired by Kofi's story, Aisha decided to explore her own emotions through art. She began to paint more freely, expressing her feelings on the canvas. Her art became a mirror of her soul, reflecting her joys, sorrows, and dreams. As she painted, she felt a sense of release and relief, as if a weight had been lifted from her shoulders. Her paintings became a visual diary of her journey, capturing moments of transformation and growth.

Aisha's art also began to attract the attention of others in her village. People were drawn to the beauty and emotion in her paintings. They found comfort and inspiration in her work, and many began to see the healing power of art for themselves. Aisha started to hold art workshops, teaching others how to use art as a tool for self-expression and healing. The workshops brought people together, creating a sense of community and support.

Through her journey, Aisha discovered that art was not just a way to pass the time, but a powerful tool for healing and connection. Her paintings became a testament to the resilience of the human spirit and the beauty of the natural world. As she continued to create, Aisha found that she had not only healed herself but had also helped others on their own journeys of self-discovery and healing.

2

Chapter 2: The Healing Power of Nature

Nature has an unparalleled ability to heal and rejuvenate the human spirit. In the bustling city of Lagos, Tunde, a stressed corporate worker, stumbled upon a hidden garden oasis. As he spent more time in the garden, he noticed his anxiety diminishing and his mind clearing. The garden's caretaker, Mama Eniola, shared her insights on the symbiotic relationship between humans and nature. Tunde learned that by nurturing the environment, he was also nurturing his own mental well-being.

Tunde's journey to the hidden garden began one stressful afternoon when he decided to take a walk to clear his mind. As he wandered through the city, he stumbled upon an overgrown pathway leading to a tranquil garden. Intrigued, he ventured inside and was greeted by the sight of blooming flowers, chirping birds, and a gentle breeze. It was a stark contrast to the chaos of the city outside.

Mama Eniola, the garden's caretaker, noticed Tunde's presence and welcomed him with a warm smile. She explained that the garden was a sanctuary for anyone seeking peace and solace. Tunde began to visit the garden regularly, finding comfort in the natural surroundings. He spent hours sitting by the pond, listening to the sounds of nature, and letting his mind unwind.

As Tunde's visits continued, Mama Eniola shared her wisdom about the healing power of nature. She explained how the garden had been a source of strength for her during difficult times. She taught Tunde how to tend to the plants, showing him the importance of nurturing the environment. Through this process, Tunde began to feel a deep connection to the natural world and a sense of responsibility for its well-being.

With each visit, Tunde felt his stress and anxiety gradually melt away. He noticed a change in his overall well-being, feeling more relaxed and rejuvenated. The garden became a place of refuge, where he could escape the pressures of his corporate job and find inner peace. He realized that by caring for the garden, he was also caring for himself.

Tunde's journey to the hidden garden transformed his perspective on life. He learned that nature had the power to heal and restore balance to the mind and body. The garden became a symbol of hope and renewal, reminding him of the importance of taking time to connect with the natural world. Tunde's story highlighted the profound impact that nature can have on mental health and well-being.

3

Chapter 3: Art as a Mirror of the Soul

Art reflects the deepest corners of the human soul. In a coastal town, Leila, a struggling writer, found herself lost in a sea of self-doubt. She attended an art exhibition where she was captivated by a series of paintings that mirrored her emotions. The artist, Madu, revealed that his work was a reflection of his own battles with depression. Through their conversations, Leila discovered the cathartic power of art and began to express her feelings through writing, finding solace in the process.

Leila's journey began when she felt overwhelmed by the pressures of her writing career. She doubted her abilities and struggled to find inspiration. One evening, she attended an art exhibition on a whim, hoping to clear her mind. As she walked through the gallery, she was struck by a series of paintings that seemed to resonate with her innermost thoughts and feelings.

The paintings depicted a range of emotions, from sorrow to joy, each one capturing a different aspect of the human experience. Leila felt a deep connection to the artwork and wanted to learn more about the artist behind it. She sought out Madu, the artist, and they began a conversation about his work. Madu explained that his paintings were a reflection of his own struggles with depression and his journey toward healing.

Inspired by Madu's honesty and vulnerability, Leila decided to explore her own emotions through writing. She started to write freely, without worrying about judgment or criticism. Her writing became a mirror of her soul, capturing her fears, hopes, and dreams. She found solace in the act of putting her thoughts on paper, and her self-doubt began to fade.

Leila's writing also began to resonate with others. She shared her work with a small group of friends, who were moved by her honesty and authenticity. Encouraged by their support, Leila continued to write, finding her voice and gaining confidence in her abilities. Her writing became a source of healing and empowerment, helping her navigate the challenges of her creative journey.

Through her conversations with Madu, Leila learned that art, in all its forms, has the power to heal and connect people. She discovered that by expressing her true self through writing, she could find clarity and purpose. Leila's story highlighted the transformative power of art and its ability to reflect the deepest corners of the human soul.

4

Chapter 4: The Silent Symphony of the Forest

The forest holds a symphony of sounds that can soothe the troubled mind. In the dense rainforests of the Amazon, a biologist named Dr. Ramos embarked on a research expedition. As he delved deeper into the forest, he noticed the calming effects of the natural sounds around him. The rustling leaves, chirping birds, and flowing rivers formed a silent symphony that eased his worries. Dr. Ramos documented his experiences, highlighting the therapeutic benefits of immersing oneself in nature.

Dr. Ramos's journey began with a mission to study the biodiversity of the rainforest. He spent his days collecting samples, observing wildlife, and recording data. However, he soon realized that the forest offered more than just scientific discoveries. The natural sounds of the forest provided a sense of tranquility that he had never experienced before. He found himself listening to the symphony of nature, from the gentle rustling of leaves to the melodic calls of birds.

As he continued his research, Dr. Ramos noticed a significant improvement in his mental well-being. The stresses and anxieties of his daily life seemed to fade away as he immersed himself in the forest. He began to document not only his scientific findings but also the therapeutic effects of the natural sounds. He recorded the sounds of the forest and played them back during moments of stress, finding that they had a calming and grounding effect.

Dr. Ramos's experiences inspired him to explore the relationship between nature and mental health. He conducted studies on the impact of natural sounds on the human mind, collaborating with psychologists and therapists. Together, they discovered that the sounds of nature could reduce stress, improve mood, and enhance cognitive function. Dr. Ramos's research highlighted the importance of preserving natural environments for their therapeutic benefits.

Through his journey, Dr. Ramos realized that the forest held a silent symphony that could heal and rejuvenate the human spirit. His story emphasized the profound connection between humans and nature, and the importance of immersing oneself in the natural world. Dr. Ramos's work inspired others to seek solace in nature and to appreciate the healing power of the silent symphony of the forest.

5

Chapter 5: The Dance of Seasons

The changing seasons mirror the ebb and flow of human emotions. In a quaint countryside, a farmer named Nneka observed the cyclical patterns of nature. She found comfort in the predictability of the seasons, each one bringing its own challenges and rewards. Through her interactions with a traveling poet, she learned to embrace the changes in her life, much like the shifting seasons. Nneka's story became a testament to the resilience of the human spirit and the wisdom found in nature's cycles.

Nneka's journey began with her daily observations of the land she farmed. She noticed how the fields changed with each season, from the vibrant colors of spring to the barren landscapes of winter. She found solace in the predictability of these cycles, knowing that after every winter, spring would come again. Her connection to the land gave her a sense of stability and resilience.

One day, a traveling poet named Kelechi visited Nneka's village. He was fascinated by the changing seasons and the stories they told. He and Nneka spent hours discussing the parallels between nature and human emotions. Kelechi shared his poetry, which captured the beauty and complexity of the seasons. Inspired by his words, Nneka began to see her own life in a new light, embracing the changes and finding strength in the cycles.

Together, Nneka and Kelechi explored the countryside, observing the subtle changes in the landscape. They found inspiration in the smallest details, from the first buds of spring to the falling leaves of autumn. Nneka began to write her own poetry, capturing her thoughts and feelings about the seasons. Her poems became a reflection of her journey, expressing her resilience and acceptance of life's changes.

Nneka's story highlighted the wisdom found in nature's cycles and the importance of embracing change. She discovered that, like the seasons, human emotions were ever-changing and that each phase had its own beauty and significance. Through her journey, Nneka learned to find peace in the ebb and flow of life, drawing strength from the natural world around her.

6

Chapter 6: The Melody of the Waves

The ocean's waves hold a timeless melody that resonates with the soul. In a coastal village, a fisherman named Olu found peace in the rhythmic sound of the waves. After a tragic accident at sea, Olu struggled with PTSD. A marine biologist named Dr. Moyo introduced him to the concept of ocean therapy. Together, they explored the therapeutic effects of the sea, from swimming in the saltwater to listening to the waves. Olu's journey of healing highlighted the profound connection between humans and the ocean.

Olu's journey began with his daily routine of fishing on the open sea. He found solace in the rhythmic sound of the waves, which provided a sense of calm and stability. However, after a traumatic accident at sea, Olu struggled with PTSD and found it difficult to return to his beloved ocean. He felt disconnected from the place that had once brought him peace.

Dr. Moyo, a marine biologist who had studied the therapeutic effects of the ocean, introduced Olu to the concept of ocean therapy. She explained how the natural elements of the sea, such as saltwater and the sound of waves, could promote healing and well-being. Olu was skeptical at first, but he agreed to give it a try.

Together, Olu and Dr. Moyo embarked on a journey of healing. They spent time swimming in the ocean, feeling the soothing effects of the saltwater on their skin. They also listened to the rhythmic sound of the waves, allowing the natural melody to calm their minds. Olu began to feel a sense of reconnection with the ocean, and his PTSD symptoms gradually diminished.

Olu's journey of healing highlighted the profound connection between humans and the ocean. He discovered that the waves held a timeless melody that could soothe the soul and promote well-being. His story emphasized the importance of exploring the natural world and finding solace in its rhythms. Olu's journey inspired others to seek out the therapeutic effects of the ocean and to appreciate the healing power of the sea.

7

Chapter 7: The Language of Flowers

Flowers have a unique language that can convey deep emotions. In a bustling metropolis, a florist named Ada used her arrangements to express her feelings. Each bouquet told a story of love, loss, and hope. One day, a customer named Chidi came to her shop seeking a bouquet for his ailing mother. Ada crafted a special arrangement that brought comfort and joy to Chidi's mother. Through her work, Ada discovered the healing power of flowers and their ability to communicate emotions beyond words.

Ada's journey began with her passion for flowers and their beauty. She loved the way each flower had its own meaning and symbolism. Her shop was filled with a variety of blooms, from roses that symbolized love to lilies that represented purity. Ada took great care in selecting the flowers for each arrangement, ensuring that they conveyed the right message.

When Chidi walked into Ada's shop, he was visibly distressed. He explained that his mother was very ill and he wanted to bring her something special to lift her spirits. Ada listened attentively and began to create a bouquet that would bring comfort and joy to Chidi's mother. She carefully chose flowers that symbolized hope, strength, and healing, and arranged them in a beautiful display.

When Chidi brought the bouquet to his mother, she was deeply touched by the gesture. The flowers brought a smile to her face and a sense of peace to her heart. Ada received a heartfelt thank you note from Chidi, expressing his gratitude for the beautiful arrangement and the comfort it brought to his mother. This experience reinforced Ada's belief in the healing power of flowers.

Ada's journey continued as she created more meaningful arrangements for her customers. She discovered that flowers had the ability to communicate emotions that words could not. Each bouquet told a story, and Ada found fulfillment in helping others express their feelings through her floral creations. Her shop became a place of solace and beauty, where people could find comfort and connection through the language of flowers.

8

Chapter 8: The Journey of the Mind

The mind's journey is a complex and intricate path. In a remote monastery, a monk named Brother John explored the depths of his consciousness through meditation and art. He created intricate mandalas that represented his inner thoughts and feelings. A visiting psychologist, Dr. Amara, studied Brother John's work and found that the process of creating mandalas had therapeutic effects on the mind. Their collaboration shed light on the intersection of art, meditation, and mental health.

Brother John's journey began with his daily practice of meditation. He found peace and clarity in the stillness of his mind, but he also wanted to express his inner experiences through art. He began to create mandalas, intricate geometric designs that symbolized the universe and the self. Each mandala was a reflection of his inner thoughts and emotions, capturing the essence of his spiritual journey.

Dr. Amara, a psychologist studying the therapeutic effects of art, visited the monastery and was fascinated by Brother John's mandalas. She observed the process of creating the mandalas and noticed the calm and focused state it induced. Dr. Amara conducted studies on the impact of mandala creation on mental health and found that it had significant therapeutic benefits. The process of creating mandalas helped to reduce stress, improve focus, and promote emotional well-being.

Through their collaboration, Brother John and Dr. Amara explored the intersection of art, meditation, and mental health. They discovered that the act of creating art could enhance the meditative experience and provide a deeper understanding of the self. Brother John's mandalas became a powerful tool for self-reflection and healing, and his work inspired others to explore the therapeutic potential of art and meditation.

Brother John's journey highlighted the complexity of the mind and the importance of exploring its depths. His story emphasized the value of combining art and meditation to promote mental health and well-being. Through his mandalas, Brother John found a way to express his inner journey and to inspire others to embark on their own paths of self-discovery and healing.

9

Chapter 9: The Symphony of the Stars

The night sky holds a symphony of stars that inspire wonder and contemplation. In a desert village, a stargazer named Zara found peace in observing the celestial bodies. Her late-night vigils under the stars became a source of comfort during difficult times. An astronomer named Dr. Malik visited the village to study the night sky and shared his knowledge with Zara. Together, they explored the therapeutic effects of stargazing and its ability to foster a sense of connection to the universe.

Zara's journey began with her fascination for the night sky. She spent countless nights lying on the desert sands, gazing up at the stars and contemplating the mysteries of the universe. The vastness of the cosmos brought her a sense of peace and wonder, allowing her to escape the challenges of her daily life. Stargazing became a meditative practice for Zara, helping her to find clarity and perspective.

Dr. Malik, an astronomer studying the night sky, visited Zara's village to conduct research. He was intrigued by Zara's passion for stargazing and invited her to join him in his observations. Together, they explored the constellations, planets, and galaxies, deepening their understanding of the universe. Dr. Malik shared his knowledge of astronomy, explaining the science behind the stars and the significance of celestial events.

Through their late-night vigils, Zara and Dr. Malik discovered the therapeutic effects of stargazing. They found that the act of observing the stars could reduce stress, promote relaxation, and foster a sense of connection to something greater than oneself. Stargazing became a way for them to find solace and inspiration, reminding them of the beauty and mystery of the universe.

Zara's journey highlighted the symphony of the stars and their ability to inspire wonder and contemplation. Her story emphasized the importance of taking time to connect with the natural world and to find peace in its rhythms. Through stargazing, Zara discovered a sense of connection to the universe and a deeper understanding of her place within it.

10

Chapter 10: The Harmony of Community

Community support plays a vital role in mental well-being. In a tight-knit neighborhood, a social worker named Amina organized art therapy sessions for residents struggling with mental health issues. The sessions brought people together, fostering a sense of belonging and mutual support. Amina's story emphasized the importance of community in promoting mental health and the healing power of collective artistic expression.

Amina's journey began with her passion for helping others. She noticed that many residents in her neighborhood were struggling with mental health issues but lacked the support they needed. Amina decided to use her background in social work and art therapy to create a space where people could come together and express themselves through art. She organized weekly art therapy sessions, inviting residents to join and share their stories.

The sessions became a safe haven for participants, providing a space where they could connect with others who understood their struggles. Amina encouraged everyone to express their emotions through various art forms, from painting to sculpting. The creative process allowed participants to explore their feelings and find a sense of release. As they shared their art and stories, a strong sense of community began to form.

Through the art therapy sessions, Amina witnessed the transformative power of collective artistic expression. Participants began to open up about their experiences, finding comfort in knowing they were not alone. The sessions fostered a sense of belonging and mutual support, helping individuals build resilience and improve their mental well-being. Amina's story highlighted the importance of community in promoting mental health and the healing potential of art.

11

Chapter 11: The Resilience of the Earth

The Earth has an incredible capacity for resilience and renewal. In a coastal city, an environmental activist named Kemi fought to protect the local wetlands from industrial pollution. She collaborated with artists to create powerful visual campaigns that raised awareness and inspired action. Kemi's journey highlighted the interconnectedness of ecological and mental well-being, showing that healing the Earth can also heal the human spirit.

Kemi's journey began with her deep love for the natural world. She was passionate about protecting the environment and was particularly concerned about the pollution affecting the local wetlands. The wetlands were a vital ecosystem, home to diverse plant and animal species, and Kemi knew that their destruction would have far-reaching consequences. She decided to take action and raise awareness about the issue.

Kemi reached out to local artists, inviting them to collaborate on a series of visual campaigns that highlighted the beauty and importance of the wetlands. The artists created stunning murals, sculptures, and installations that captured the essence of the ecosystem and the threats it faced. The visual campaigns garnered significant attention, sparking conversations and inspiring community members to take action.

Through her activism, Kemi discovered the resilience of the Earth and its capacity for renewal. She saw how the wetlands began to recover as more people joined the efforts to protect them. Kemi also noticed a positive shift in her own mental well-being. The act of working to heal the Earth brought her a sense of purpose and fulfillment, reinforcing the idea that ecological and mental health are deeply interconnected.

Kemi's journey emphasized the importance of environmental activism and the powerful impact it can have on both the planet and the human spirit. Her story inspired others to become advocates for the Earth, showing that by healing the environment, we can also heal ourselves.

12

Chapter 12: The Soul of the Soil

The soil holds the soul of the Earth, nurturing life and fostering growth. In a rural farming community, a young agriculturist named Femi implemented sustainable farming practices that revitalized the land. He shared his knowledge with fellow farmers, emphasizing the importance of caring for the soil. Femi's story concluded the journey through art, mental health, and ecological awakening, illustrating the profound connection between humans and the environment.

Femi's journey began with his fascination for agriculture and the natural world. He studied sustainable farming practices and was determined to implement them in his community. Femi noticed that the soil in his village had become depleted due to unsustainable farming methods, leading to reduced crop yields and declining soil health. He knew that restoring the soil was essential for the long-term well-being of the community and the environment.

Femi began by experimenting with organic fertilizers, crop rotation, and cover cropping. He observed how these practices improved the soil's fertility and structure, leading to healthier plants and higher yields. Femi's success inspired him to share his knowledge with other farmers in the community. He organized workshops and demonstrations, teaching sustainable farming techniques and emphasizing the importance of caring for the soil.

As more farmers adopted these practices, the community saw a significant improvement in crop yields and soil health. Femi's efforts revitalized the land, creating a more sustainable and resilient farming system. He also noticed a positive impact on the mental well-being of the farmers. The act of working with the soil and seeing the fruits of their labor brought a sense of fulfillment and connection to the Earth.

Femi's journey highlighted the profound connection between humans and the environment. His story illustrated the importance of caring for the soil, which holds the soul of the Earth and nurtures life. Femi's efforts to promote sustainable farming practices concluded the journey through art, mental health, and ecological awakening, showing that by nurturing the environment, we can also nurture our own well-being.

"Soul of the Soil: A Journey Through Art, Mental Health, and Ecological Awakening"

In a world where the hustle and bustle often overshadow our inner selves and the natural world, "Soul of the Soil" embarks on a profound journey to reconnect us with the essence of life. Through the intertwined themes of art, mental health, and ecological awakening, this book weaves captivating stories that illustrate the deep connections between these facets of human existence.

Meet Aisha, a young artist who discovers the healing power of painting in her serene mountain village. Follow Tunde, a stressed corporate worker, as he finds solace in a hidden garden oasis in Lagos. Leila, a struggling writer, learns to express her deepest emotions through art, inspired by a fellow artist's journey. Dr. Ramos, a biologist, uncovers the therapeutic benefits of the silent symphony of the rainforest, while Nneka, a farmer, draws strength from the changing seasons.

Explore the timeless melody of the waves with Olu, a fisherman healing from trauma, and witness the language of flowers through Ada, a florist in a bustling metropolis. Journey with Brother John, a monk creating intricate mandalas, and Zara, a stargazer finding peace in the symphony of the stars. Discover the power of community support through Amina's art therapy sessions and the resilience of the Earth with Kemi, an environmental activist. Finally, join Femi, an agriculturist revitalizing the land with sustainable farming practices.

"Soul of the Soil" is a heartwarming and thought-provoking exploration of how art, nature, and community can guide us toward healing, renewal, and a deeper understanding of our place in the world. Through these inspiring stories, readers are invited to reflect on their own journeys and find solace in the interconnectedness of life.